RATTAN FURNITURE

Tropical Comfort Throughout the House

HARVEY SCHWARTZ

CONTENTS

TROPICAL ORIGINS

THE RATTAN PLANT

Rattan is a plant in the palm family which grows in tropical jungles. The largest source today is still the Philippines. Tough, solid stems of palasan rattan vary from one to two inches in diameter and grow as vines 200 to 500 feet in length. When harvested, rattan is cut into 13-foot lengths and the dry sheathing is removed. The stems are sun-dried and stored for seasoning. These long poles are straightened, graded by diameter and quality (judged by the inter-node spacing, fewer nodes is better),and shipped to furniture-making factories.

Rattan is almost impervious, but light-weight and easy to handle. It will withstand extreme conditions of humidity and temperature and has a natural resistance to bug damage.

Unlike rattan, bamboo is a hollow grass with horizontal growth ridges along its stems. Bamboo was used to build charming small furniture in the late nineteenth- and early twentieth-century in various tropical places. Some bamboo furniture includes stronger and smoother rattan poles.Examples of furniture made with bamboo can be found in the sections Rattan on the Porch and Rattan in the Hallway in this book

CONSTRUCTION OF RATTAN FURNITURE

When constructing furniture from rattan, the long poles are boiled, steamed, or torched until they are pliable. Then the poles are bent into molds and nailed at the joints. When they are dry, they hold their forms lashed together with long, flat, and thin wrapping fiber, called bury,in neat and intricate patterns. Sometimes the spaces between tightly stacked poles are filled with thin, round sica vine, which itself is used as decorative supporting material. Furniture made from rattan should endure the hard knocks of everyday living and last a lifetime. Rattan will not be ruined when exposed to rain and sun, so it has gained popularity for outdoor furniture.

Above & following page: Color pictures of the manufacturing process at Tai Shin Handicraft Co., Ltd., Taiwan, R.O.C., 1983, with a showroom at Tai Shin International, Inc., 18560 Vincennes St., Northridge, California 91324. Tai Shin was established in 1969 and moved to a larger warehouse in 1980.

The best quality rattan furniture has these features:

• intricate bends, the more the better. Pretzel and related variations command the highest prices.

• many poles tightly stacked, ranging from two poles in more common forms to twelve poles, which are nearly impossible to find today. The most sought-after rattan has six stacked poles.

• few blemishes such as dark spots or stem nodes

• well wrapped joints which add beauty to the pieces

• the older the better

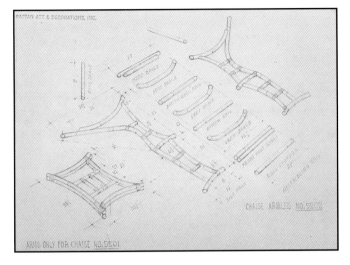

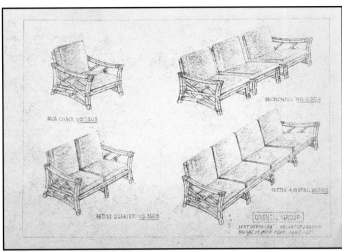

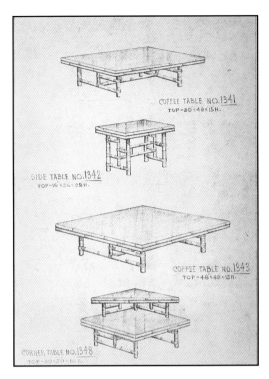

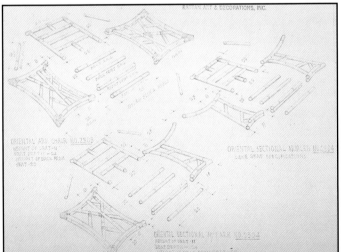

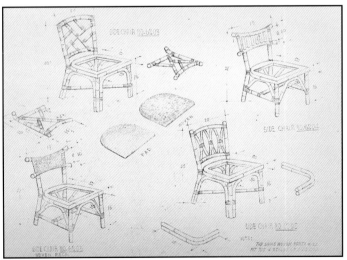

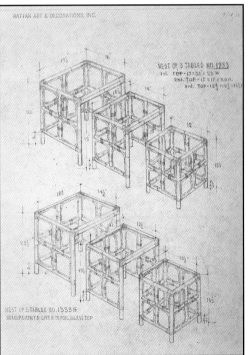

Blueprint drawings of rattan furniture from Rattan Art & Decorations, Inc., Manila, Philippines, made for the Tropical Sun Rattan Company of Pasadena, California.

Corner detail of a rectangular rattan table with wrapping.

Left: Detail of the wrapping of a table joint.

Below center & right: Two details of old chair construction with beautifully wrapped end of an arm.

Detail of a pre-World War II rattan arm chair having two large and one small rattan strand on the continuous arms and back. Sica vertical ribs run separately in the back and seat.

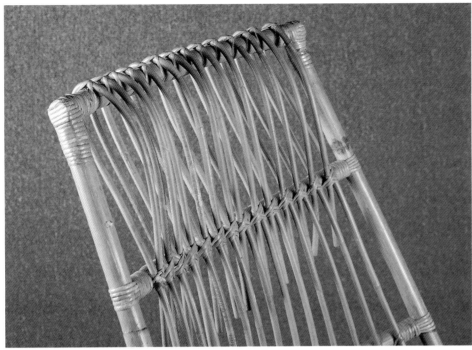

Back detail of a large rattan rocking arm chair with continuous sica ribs curving from the back through the seat.

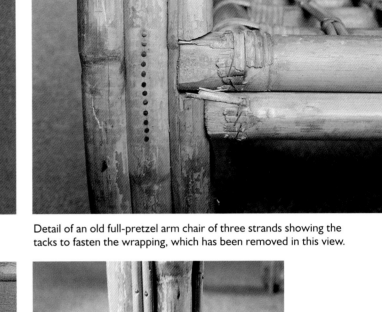

Detail of an old full-pretzel arm chair of three strands showing the tacks to fasten the wrapping, which has been removed in this view.

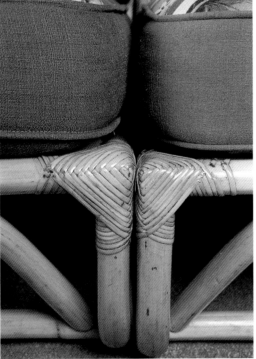

Far left: Detail of the old wrapping on a leg and supporting rattan pole.

Center: A perfect three-corner wrapping on a sectional settee.

Left: Detail of a stacked rattan table leg showing old wrapping and normal wear.

11

DESIGN CHANGES IN RATTAN FURNITURE

When the British Empire was at its height in the nineteenth century, popularity for bamboo and related tropical furniture was high. Families stationed in the tropics and the Orient returned to England with furniture mementos that actually were highly unsuitable to the cool English climate, but held up well in it nevertheless. Forms of rattan were included in this group, particularly small and portable tables, chairs, and decorative hall pieces.

During the early decades of the twentieth century, rattan furniture made primarily in the Philippine islands remained a curious oddity known best in Europe and America to travelers who encountered its practicality in the tropics. The designs of the 1920s, '30s, and '40s reflected the Victorian tropical styles. When American movies began to include rattan in many of the outdoor scenes, its popularity began to rise for home use. It became the chief type of furniture for the homes of U.S. Army and Navy personnel in the Pacific islands during World War II.

During the 1940s, while California's population was growing and popular movies were produced in Hollywood, furniture designers such as Paul Frankel began to make new designs for rattan furniture. Frankel designed the square pretzel arm with a dip at the arm rest. In the period 1949 to 1951, squared-off corners were common on rattan furniture.

Companies such as Tropical Sun Rattan in Pasadena, California, and Seven Seas, also in California, sold large quantities of new rattan for indoor and outdoor use. At Tropical Sun Rattan, one man alone made samples of designs to be mass produced for forty-eight years; his name was Howard, and he was referred to as Howard-the-sample-maker. An example of one of his sample pretzel arm chairs is found on page 39.

tropical furniture for the modern home

Top Quality RATTAN

BAUGHMAN FURNITURE FACTORY

PEÑAFRANCIA & STO. SEPULCRO STS., MANILA, PHILIPPINES   CABLE ADDRESS: BAUFURN MANILA

Above right: Cover of the catalog for the Baughman Furniture Factory, Manila, Philippines, c. 1940. Baughman made top grade and high line rattan only.

Right: Dark stained serving table attributed to California designer Paul Frankel, c. 1945, with rectangular mahogany top over a case with two cupboards flanking three drawers, resting on black rattan legs. $2700.

In the 1950s, Don Loper, along with other designers and architects in Hollywood, made innovative designs for rattan in home and office use. Herbert Ritts introduced time-saving construction details, such as s-shaped springs for cushion supports and the use of colored gimp instead of bury rattan wrap, which lowered the cost of the furniture.

Unfortunately, the very innovations designed to save money in production costs may also have doomed the industry to decline in the late 1950s and 1960s, as new rattan was perceived to be inferior and it fell out of vogue. Tropical Sun Rattan shifted its furniture lines to metal furniture and awnings.

Label for the Ritts Co. of Los Angeles, reading "Ritts Co. Original Fine Casual Furniture, Los Angeles, 64," as found on a 1940s bar stool.

Tropical Sun Rattan showroom, November, 1946.

Catalog "Rattan Furniture at its best! by F. Debski, Inc., New York City."

Far left: Catalog of the Tropical Sun Rattan Company, Pasadena, California, c. 1955, operating from about 1955 to 1979.

Left: Information sheet from Tropical Sun Rattan with 28 room arrangement ideas.

Lower left: Catalog for Tropical Sun Rattan, c. 1970.

Lower right: Cover of the 1977 catalog "Tropical Sun Company, Importers and Manufacturers of Genuine Smart Philippine Rattan Furniture, Rugs and Accessories, 111 W. Colorado Blvd., Pasadena, CA."

Letterhead for Tropical Sun Company.

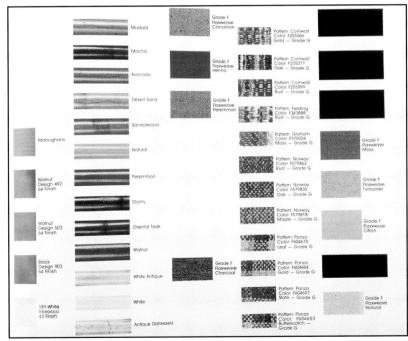

Page from the 1977 catalog for the Tropical Sun Company showing the different wood finishes and three upholstery fabric types that could be ordered: *Canvas* (least expensive), *Flaxweave* (medium expensive), and *Herculon* (most expensive).

Catalog "Rattan Furniture for Export, Best Materials, Finest Workmanship, Prompt Service, Made in Hong Kong."

Thin paper catalog for rattan manufacturer "Fook Loon, Hong Kong."

Letterhead for Harvey's and Tropical Sun Rattan, 1979.

The Most Unusual Collection Of **ART DECO**, **RATTAN** Art Nouveau Antiques And Jewlery.

HARVEY'S +
TROPICAL SUN RATTAN
7365-67 MELROSE AVE.
LOS ANGELES, CA. 90046
(213) 857-1991

THE FAN ARM. ©

Visit our new prop shop!

Above: Catalog of Tropi-Cal, 5716 Alba Street, Los Angeles.

Right: Catalog of Tropi-Cal, 5716 Alba Street, Los Angeles.

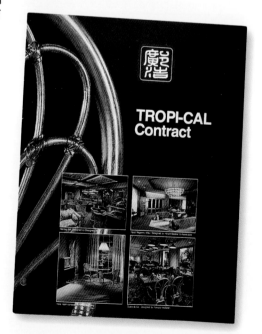

TROPI-CAL Contract

HARVEY'S
& TROPICAL SUN RATTAN
20's THRU 50's FURNITURE & ACCESSORIES

As seen on "The Golden Girls"

7365 MELROSE AVE.
LA 90046 (213) 857-1991

Above: Advertisement for Harvey's and Tropical Sun featuring the fan-arm design.

Left: Advertisement for Harvey's and Tropical Sun, "As Seen on `The Golden Girls'," dated October 31, 1987.

Retail shop interior showing rattan furniture from Ralph Stein of Hudson, Inc., 115 West 23rd Street, New York City.

DECORATING WITH RATTAN

During the 1950s, the building boom in Arizona included housing tracts that were furnished largely with new rattan furniture because it was perfectly suited to the desert climate. Across the country, many home owners added "California" or "Florida" rooms to their homes and furnished them with rattan.

People traveled in increasing numbers to Hawaii and other tropical locations on luxury ocean liners during the 1950s. On board, they received menus with attractively decorated covers, some designed by prominent artists specifically for the cruise lines. Once the travelers returned home, many menu covers became framed and mounted on the walls of their tropical rooms.

Artwork and pictures with tropical themes were usually displayed with rattan furniture in manufacturers' showrooms. The colorful and casual themes they represent blend perfectly with rattan.

TROPICAL PRINT FABRICS: JUST RIGHT WITH RATTAN

The cushions on rattan chairs, sofas, and lounge chairs have traditionally been covered with tropical print fabrics, many of bark cloth with textured surface. Beautiful colors and bird and floral designs are stunning accompaniments to the natural wood surface of the furniture. Rattan manufacturers ordered their yard goods in large quantities from fabric houses like Spectrum in New York. But even home sewers could find an assortment in their mail-order catalogs from Montgomery Ward, Sears, and the like.

Looms 48 inches wide produced cloth with 26-inch design repeats. Using these standard dimensions, rattan manufacturers usually made their seats 22 inches wide (allowing for a one-inch seam on both sides).

Page from a mail order catalog showing fabric yard goods typically used in the 1930-1960s period to make the cushion covers for rattan furniture.

Fabric yard goods typically used for the cushions on rattan furniture and draperies, c. 1940s-1970s.

Above: Print fabric with white birds and swirling background, designed and manufactured by Spectrum, New York, 1949, was made in six different color combinations; four of them are shown here.

Right: Aloha shirt made with upholstry fabric manufactured by Spectrum, New York, c. 1950, labeled Wong's Drapery Shoppe, Honolulu, Hawaii.

RATTAN HAS A COMEBACK

In the 1980s, renewed interest in contemporary rattan was noted in the furniture markets. A designer named McGuire made reproduction rattan that was sold at the Pacific Design Center in Los Angeles. Business that had lagged for decades made a slow comeback in response to the growing awareness of a "California look" in sets for movies and television shows that used rattan in many of the scenes. In the 1980s, the popular television program "The Golden Girls" showed rattan furniture from the author on the set. This influenced many people in the television audience subtly and gradually to like rattan furniture and want it in their own homes. Public rooms in restaurants and hotels were also furnished with rattan when a nautical or tropical theme was required.

RATTAN ON THE PORCH

Rattan swivel and rocking arm chair on round base of seven horizontal rattan bands. $695.

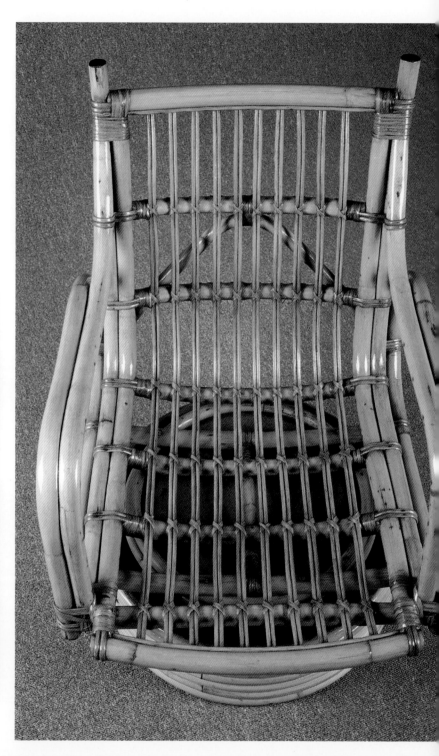

Left: Floor lamp with lantern-style shade, rattan stem, and reed mat covering near the round base. $595.

Center: Contemporary octagonal low table of bamboo with pieced bamboo frame and geometric/round design below glass top (missing), supported on eight arches and straight bamboo legs. $175.

Right: Large rattan rocking arm chair with continuous sica ribs curving from the back through the seat. The arms are bent to form the rockers. This chair was custom made for someone over seven feet tall.

Above: Rectangular rattan table with wood veneer top over a smaller shelf and skirt and sides of parallel sica. $595.

Right: 1930s stick rattan arm chair with orange cushions. $1100.

Far right: Old bamboo magazine rack retaining Oriental painted panels, two on the sides and one on the low shelf. Near the top is a rectangular cage open at the top with bamboo side construction. $425.

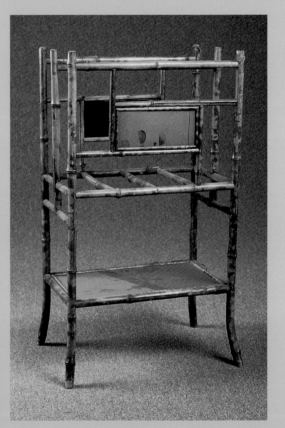

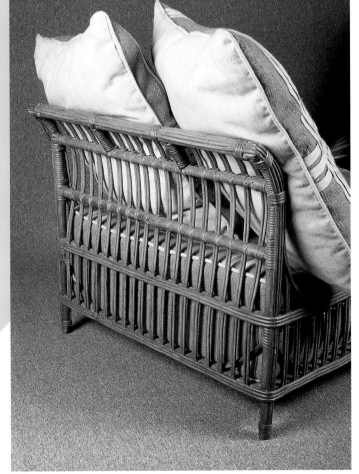

Left: Rattan and sica end table with three staggered mahogany shelves on parallel upright

Below left & right: Daybed of rattan with vertical openwork ends and skirt, beige and white pillows. $2200.

AboveL Set of three contemporary graduated stacking tables with square tops of split bamboo and bamboo legs with side decorations. $175 the set.

Left: Old rattan stepped rectangular end table of painted red and black sections. The three shelves are graduated in size with vertical pairs of thin rattan on the long sides and a curved transition between the middle and lower shelves. $565.

Two folding chairs of thin rattan with bamboo frames. $75.

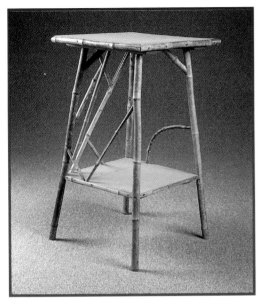

Old bamboo square end table with solid wood top and shelf covered in grass cloth and four straight bamboo legs with thin bamboo side pieces of ornamental use. $425.

Folding side chair with rattan frame and thin rattan in the back panel. $50.

Nice contemporary bamboo arm chair of Chinese style with arched and vertical bamboo paneled back, arched arms, cushioned back and seat, deep skirt, and bamboo legs joined by a framing six-sided stretcher. $325.

Old bamboo table with octagonal lacquered top of Oriental floral design in bamboo frame resting on three straight bamboo legs with three intersecting braces. $375.

Old bamboo sewing table with pine or cedar box covered in grass mat with hinged lid. The front of the compartment has an applied, five-point decoration of cut bamboo. Four raking bamboo legs are joined by a mat-covered shelf. $425.

Above: Arm chair with cushioned back and seat, designed by Henry Olko, 1981.

Right: Small old bamboo shelf unit with two long and two short shelves, grass mat covering on four bamboo legs with occasional bamboo decorative pieces. $300.

Below: Arm chair of stacked rattan with cushioned back and seat sold by Tropi-Cal, Los Angeles.

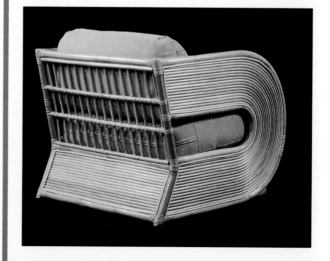

RATTAN IN THE HALLWAY

Pre-World War II
room setting from
Rattan Art &
Decorations, Inc.,
2957 Herran Santa
Ana, Manila, P.I.

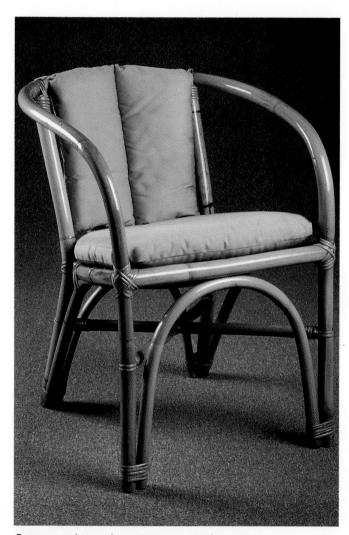

Left: Round mirror in frame comprised of three strands of one-inch thick rattan poles. $450.

Below: Half round console table with light wooden top and rattan frame and supports with a decorative looped design shelf of rattan and sica. $565

Rattan arm chair with continuous curving legs, arms, and back, with back and seat cushions and raking back legs, arched braces, and crossing stretcher. $375.

Color print of a watercolor painting depicting a Chinese landscape. $35.

Above: Old bamboo writing desk with three-shelf unit above a square grass mat covered table top, one drawer in the skirt with grass mat front resting on four splayed bamboo legs joined by a shaped shelf with grass mat covering. $975.

Right: Old bamboo hall stand with four coat hooks and rectangular mirrored panel on woven wicker back, with projecting bamboo umbrella or cane stand. $1100.

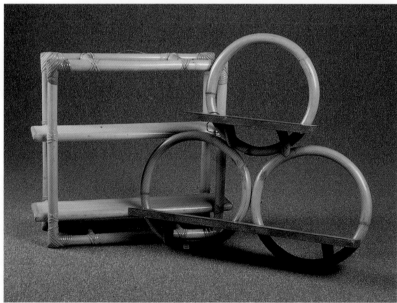

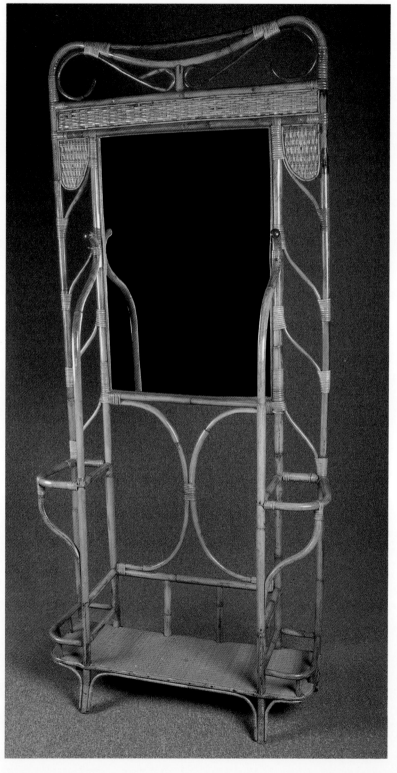

Top: Rectangular table with mahogany veneered top, plastic wrap, and open stretchers. $285.

Above: Hanging shelf with two dark Formica shelves. $275. Standing or hanging shelf rack with two light Formica shelves. $185.

Right: Ornate rattan hall stand with large rectangular mirrored panel in back and two side cane or umbrella stands. $2200.

Left: Old bamboo standing shelf unit with three short and three long shelves supported by four main bamboo poles at the corners and applied, decorative bamboo pieces. $775.

Above: Old bamboo rectangular table with grass covered overhanging top and smaller shelf on four raking bamboo legs with corner bracing. $375.

Right: Contemporary standing coat rack with ball finial and smaller balls on two slanted arms, central pole, and round base. $375.

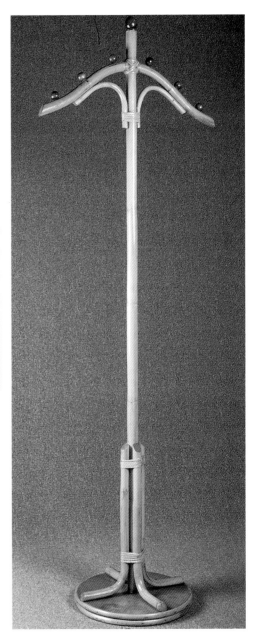

Above: Contemporary bamboo corner table with one square corner and a rounded front, joined by split bamboo pieces. The top rests on three straight bamboo legs and conforming stretchers. $225.

Left: Color print of a watercolor painting of Chinese fishermen. $35.

Contemporary rectangular rattan dining/library table with mahogany top with rattan edge over a woven skirt and end panels of woven rattan that form the supports. $395.

Octagonal table with grass mat covering, resting on four bamboo legs of clustered pieces joined by a crossing stretcher. $300.

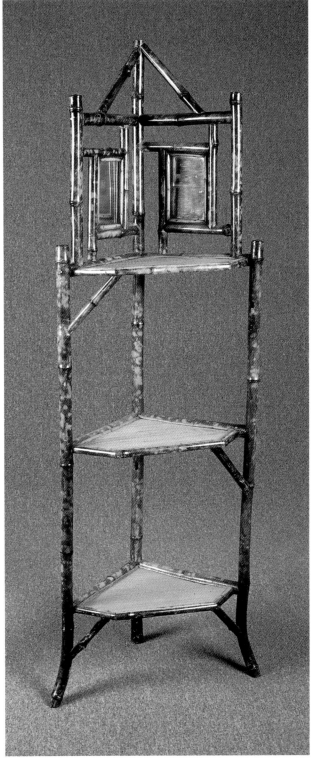

Bamboo corner shelf unit with two back panels with mirrored plates over three shelves of five sides with grass mat surface supported on three bamboo legs. $475.

Print of net fishermen signed Can White,
in woven mat and bamboo frame. $375.

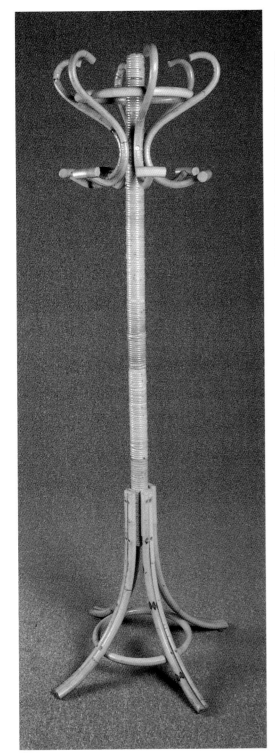

Far left: Contemporary coat rack with six s-hooks on a tall wrapped rattan pole with four bent legs.

Left: Old bamboo five-shelf unit with knob finials on bamboo corner posts and bamboo back panel, five shaped shelves of wood with ribbed, conforming supports. $775.

Below: Old rectangular table with stamped and pieced leather covering of purple floral design within an applied frame. The top rests on four straight legs joined by a lacquered shelf with floral design and spindle skirt. $175.

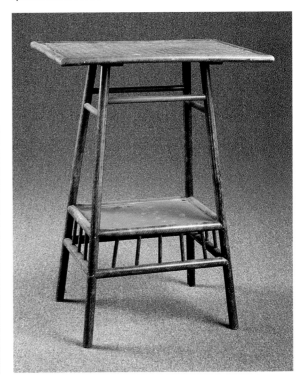

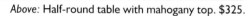

Above: Half-round table with mahogany top. $325.

Right: Miniature rattan half round table with grass mat on top and four rattan legs with thin rattan stretcher. $125.

Below: Hanging rattan shelf unit with two short and two long shelves, curved ends with rattan clusters, mirrored back missing. $600.

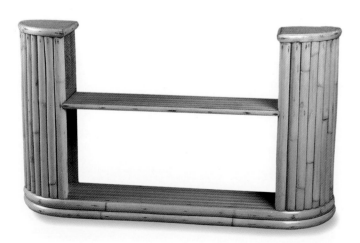

Old bamboo umbrella stand with two framed panels (now empty) in the back and four uprights framing a rectangular space with horizontal braces near the top and bottom. $285.

Color print of a watercolor painting
of a Chinese fisherman. $35.

Above: Old bamboo ornate hall stand with rectangular back, five hat supports around a diamond-shaped mirrored panel and mat frame, with projecting cane or umbrella holder. $1100.

Right: Old rattan hall stand with three hat hooks and a rectangular mirrored panel in back, two slanted panels with rattan mat covering and projecting cane or umbrella stand. $1600.

RATTAN IN THE LIVING ROOM

Living room setting from
Tropical Sun Rattan,
Pasadena, California.

Above & right: Three-strand full pretzel arm chair with an adjustable back and pastel flamingo fabric on the cushions. This chair was made by Howard-the-sample-maker for Tropical Sun Rattan Co., Pasadena, around 1947. $1100.

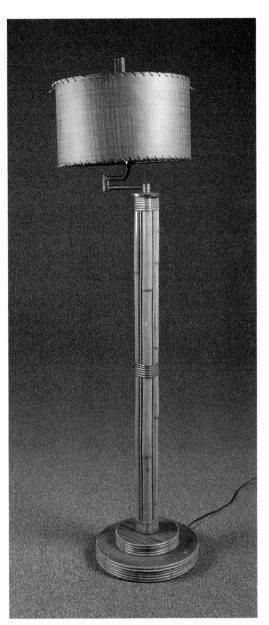

Floor lamp with round green parchment shade, bending iron arm, stacked rattan stem, and stepped round base. $575.

Two prints of tropical dancers signed Gill. $450 each.

Far left: Fabric yard goods with flamingo design typically used for the cushions on rattan furniture and draperies, c. 1940s-1970s.

Above: Old full pretzel arm chair of three strands.

Left: Small round table with cane handle, laminated top and plastic wrap, round base. $175

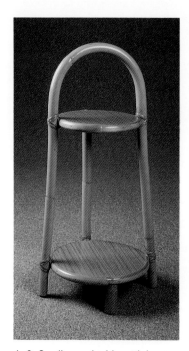

Left: Small round table with bent rattan frame and wood grain Formica top and shelf. $150.

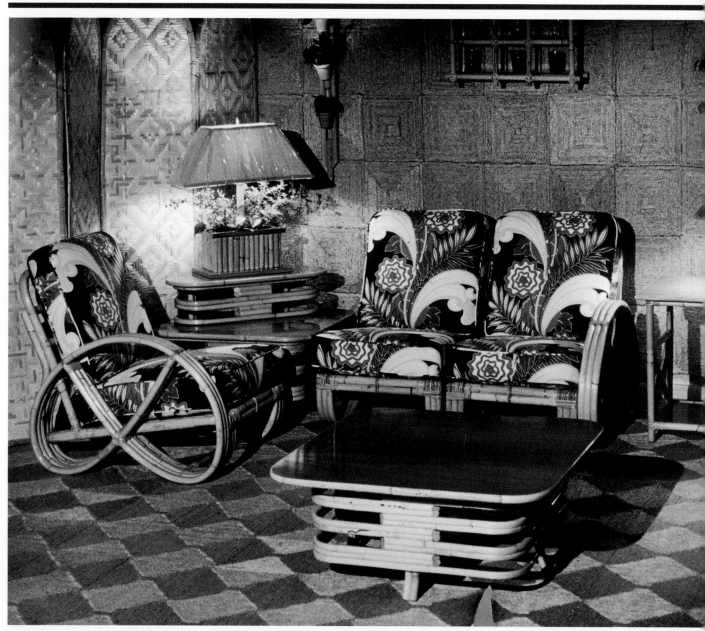

1938 living room setting from Tropical Sun Rattan, Pasadena, California.

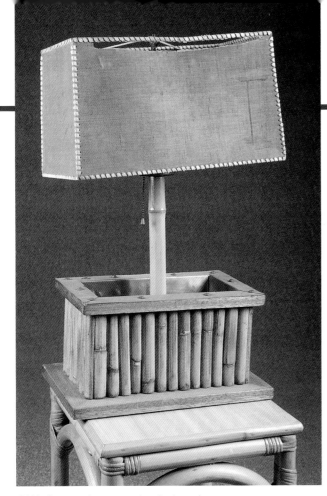

Table lamp with rectangular shade and rattan post resting in a rectangular, copper-lined plant container faced with rattan. $375.

Above: Coffee table with mahogany veneer top overhanging the stacked rattan square base. $595.

Left: Side table with triangular shelf over square top, rattan trim and feet. $795.

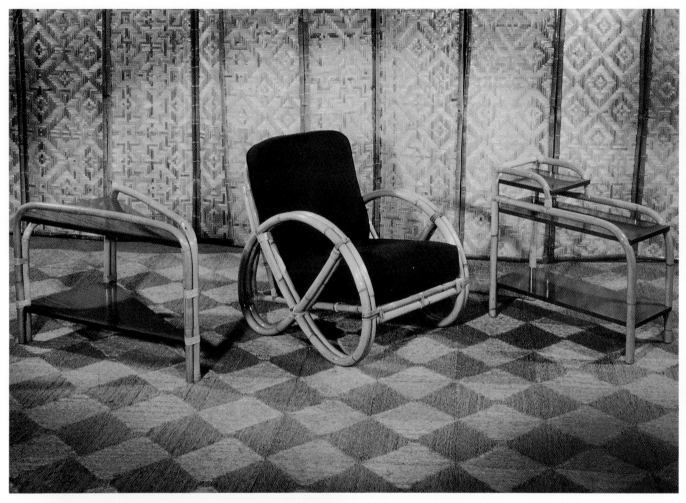

Above: 1938 living room setting from Tropical Sun Rattan, Pasadena, California.

Left: Triangular end table with mahogany veneer top and shelf on three rattan legs. $295.

Left: Fabric yard goods with floral design typically used for the cushions on rattan furniture and draperies, c. 1940s-1970s.

Above: Three-part sofa with three-strand, pretzel-bent rattan ends, cushions with black background and green leaf design. This is an example of a three-strand, "standard" 3/4-pretzel design. $2000.

Right: Living room setting from Tropical Sun Rattan, Pasadena, California.

Pre-World War II living room setting from Rattan Art &
Decorations, Inc., 2957 Herran Santa Ana, Manila, P.I.

46

Top left: Round drum coffee table with mahogany top and circular rattan supports stacked.

Above: Watercolor painting of a flamingo signed Shirrell Graves, in mat and frame. This artist's work was widely displayed and sold in rattan furniture showrooms. $1250.

Left: Living room setting from Tropical Sun Rattan, Pasadena, California.

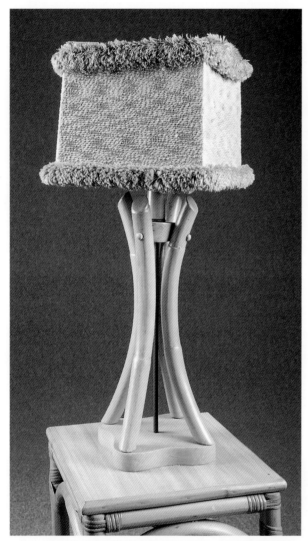

Above: Table lamp with tan shade with fringe trim on four raking legs and rounded square base. $245.

Above right: Round end table with mahogany top and rattan legs joined by three rattan rings and crossing stretcher. $295.

Right: Rattan hanging shelf with four stacked rattan frame and two mahogany shelves. $295.

Left: Fabric yard goods with floral design typically used for the cushions on rattan furniture and draperies, c. 1940s-1970s.

Above: Two six-strand square pretzel arm chairs (knock-offs of a design by Paul Frankel) and a low, round drum table. Chairs $895 each.

Right: Round end table with mahogany top and shelf with rattan supports. This table is early with lots of wrapping.

Above: Living room setting from Tropical Sun Rattan, Pasadena, California.

Right: Table lamp with parchment shade with black line dots, stacked rattan stem, and round mahogany base. $325.

Framed painting of a white bird and red flower, signed Seay, an artist for Turner Manufacturing. $595.

Six-strand rattan arm chair with square pretzel arms, straight back and high stacked base, with pastel flamingo fabric covered cushions. $1000

Rectangular end table with short mahogany shelf over projecting mahogany shelf and stacked rattan base.

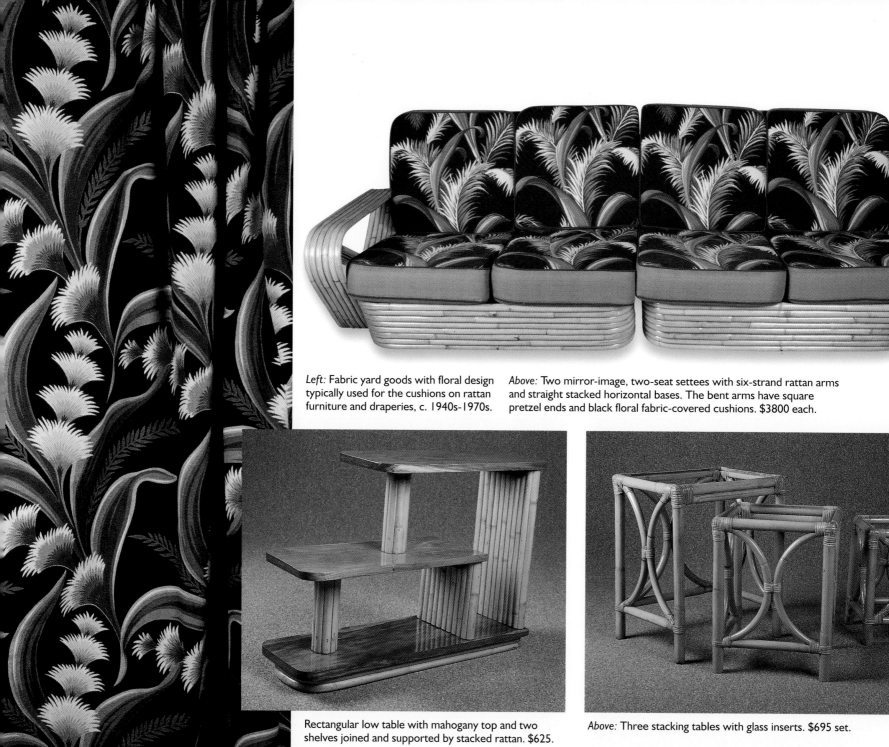

Left: Fabric yard goods with floral design typically used for the cushions on rattan furniture and draperies, c. 1940s-1970s.

Above: Two mirror-image, two-seat settees with six-strand rattan arms and straight stacked horizontal bases. The bent arms have square pretzel ends and black floral fabric-covered cushions. $3800 each.

Rectangular low table with mahogany top and two shelves joined and supported by stacked rattan. $625.

Above: Three stacking tables with glass inserts. $695 set.

Opposite: Pre-World War II living room setting from Rattan Art & Decorations, Inc., 2957 Herran Santa Ana, Manila, P.I.

54

Living room setting from Tropical Sun Rattan, Pasadena, California.

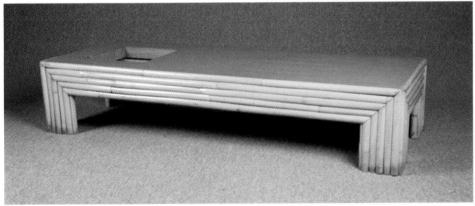

Opposite: Pre-World War II living room setting from Rattan Art & Decorations, Inc., 2957 Herran Santa Ana, Manila, P.I.

Top: Two-seat rattan settee with stacked poles for horizontal arms and base, with gray fabric covered cushions. Notice the tight bends for the arms. $3000.

Above: Very long mahogany and rattan coffee table with rectangular top and a rectangular opening near one end for a planter. $475.

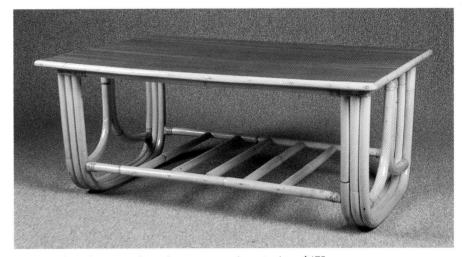

Coffee table with rectangular mahogany top and curving legs. $475.

Above: Rattan arm chair from Ritts Company of Los Angeles with coiled springs under the seat and plastic wrap, arched back with three rattan ribs, and three-strand curving arms. $495.

Two at right: Fabric yard goods with floral design typically used for the cushions on rattan furniture and draperies, c. 1940s-1970s.

Above: Living room setting from the Baughman Furniture Factory, Manila, Philippines, c. 1940.

Right: Living room setting from Tropical Sun Rattan, Pasadena, California.

Below: Coffee table with rectangular mahogany top and shelf and three-strand bent rattan legs and frame of un-peeled poles. $500.

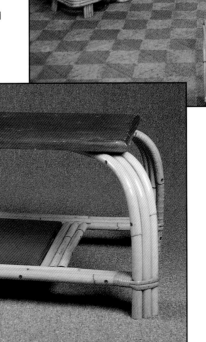

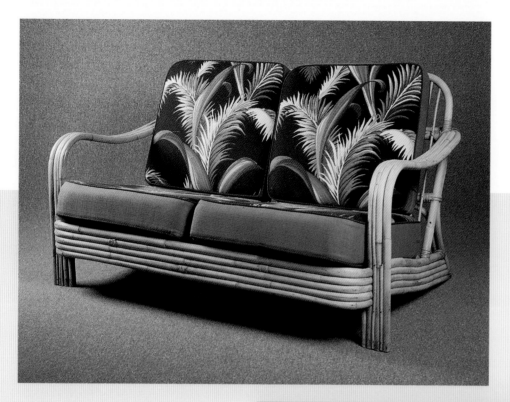

Above: Pre-World War II rattan two-seat settee with three-strand rattan arms, five horizontal skirt strands curved to hold the cushions in and so nicknamed the "wave base," and cushions with black floral print fabric.

Right: Rattan arm chair made by Tropical Sun Rattan Co. with four strands and leopard print cushions. This is from boxed, unused, new stock.

Far right: Table lamp with burlap round shade and stacked rattan stem on stepped round mahogany base. $325.

58

Living room setting from
Tropical Sun Rattan,
Pasadena, California.

Pair of watercolor pictures in bamboo style-frames,
signed GET 1941, showing an Asian woman with a
basket and an Asian man carrying cut reeds. $275.

Above: Low arm chair with continuous curving back and arms, cushion for seat missing. $425.

Above right: Large rattan fireplace surround custom made for actor Gary Cooper's home in the 1930s.

Left: Table lamp with green parchment rectangular shade and ring with cylinder and silk flowers, on a round base. $175

Fabric yard goods with floral design typically used for the cushions on rattan furniture and draperies, c. 1940s-1970s.

Rattan sectional settees with a three-strand, open-square arm. Placed together they form a two-seat settee.

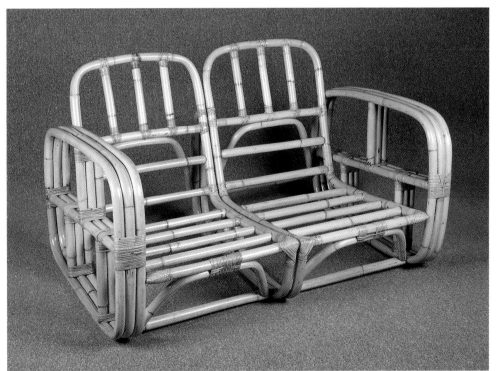

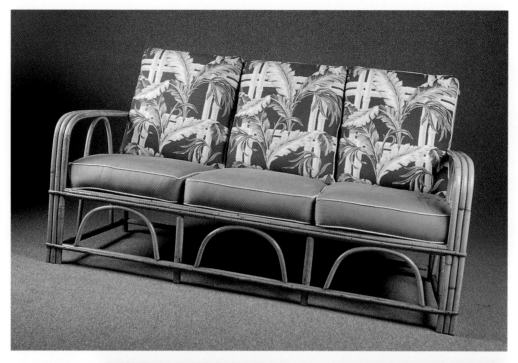

Above: Three-seat rattan settee with straight back and sixteen vertical ribs, three-strand arms and straight legs joined by straight box stretchers. Floral back cushions and dark pink seat cushions. $1825.

Right: Pair of rattan arm chairs with orange cushioned seats and original green floral back cushions. $695 each.
Standing floor lamp with round double shade and three spider legs on ring base. $895.

Coffee table and fish tank with four-strand rattan top frame and central dome-shaped Plexiglas section containing sand and sea shells. All this rests on a round rattan base. $1200.

Low rectangular table with mahogany top and curved rattan supports joined by straight rattan poled shelf. $525.

Drum table with round mahogany top on a cylindrical base faced with horizontal rattan. $575.

63

Opposite: Pre-World War II living room setting from Rattan Art & Decorations, Inc., 2957 Herran Santa Ana, Manila, P.I.

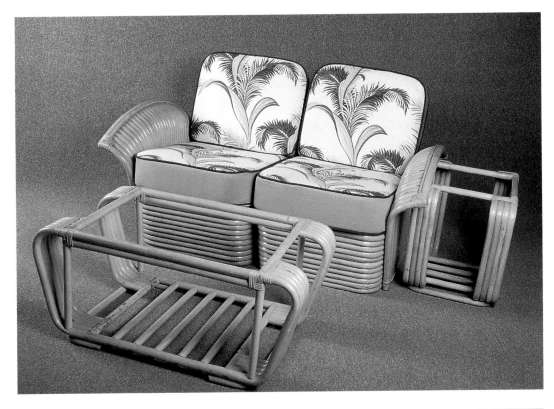

Above: Rattan two-seat, fan arm settee, with a coffee table and a side table with glass tops.

Right: Rattan chair with fan arms, stacked base, and cushioned back and seat covered in fabric with black background and green fern design.

Far right: Fabric yard goods with swag and leaf design typically used for the cushions on rattan furniture and draperies, c. 1940s-1970s.

Above & top right: Pre-World War II rattan fan-arm chair with horizontal stacked base and cushions with black and pink floral cushions. The two arms are bolted to the back and base; this is a knock-down piece. Notice the fine tapering done by hand on each pole of the arms. $1800.

Right: Low round table with mahogany top and four pair of curved rattan supports joined by a circular stretcher.

Above: Drum table with pony skin top and stacked rattan base. $695.

Right: Contemporary hanging rattan shelf unit with three rectangular grass mat covered shelves and thin rattan ornaments. $75.

Newspaper photograph showing Cuban Dictator Fulgencio Batista dancing next to a fan-arm chair.

Opposite: Pre-World War II living room setting from Rattan Art & Decorations, Inc., 2957 Herran Santa Ana, Manila, P.I.

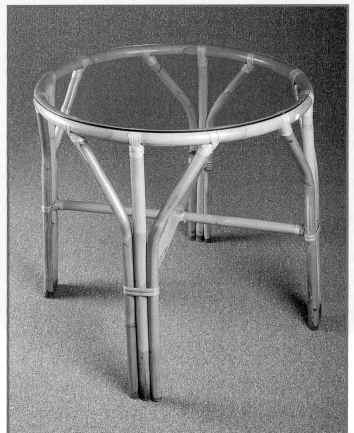

Left: Table lamp with parchment shade and three rattan stems on a mahogany base. $275.

Above: Contemporary round rattan table with four stacked legs joined by a crossing stretcher and round glass top. $275.

Right: Rattan magazine rack with heavy, thick rattan. $225.

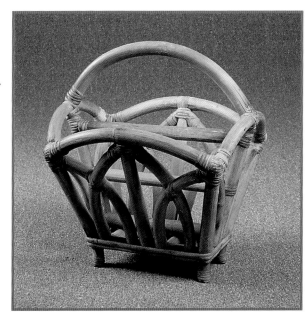

Left: Living room setting from Tropical Sun Rattan, Pasadena, California.

Right: Fabric yard goods with floral design typically used for the cushions on rattan furniture and draperies, c. 1940s-1970s.

Below: Two-seat settee of rattan with double horseshoe, four-strand arms, straight back with five horizontal ribs, with green floral cushions. $2500.

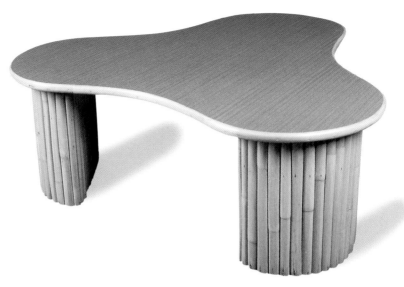

Above: Amoeba-shaped low table with brown, wood-grain Formica top and rounded corners on three vertical stacked legs. $895.

Left: Three-panel folding screen of carefully planned wicker panels wherein the knots in the reeds form repeating geometric patterns. $595.

Below: Four-strand, double-horseshoe arm chair with gray floral and black cushions.

71

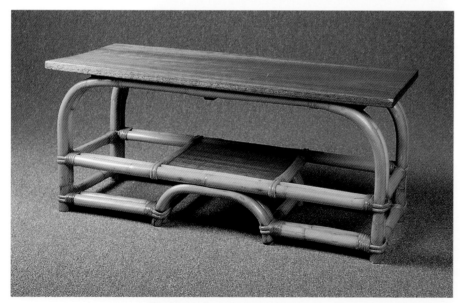

Top: Rattan three-strand, three-quarter, reverse-bent-pretzel arm chair with rounded back, seat with coil spring supports for the cushions. Beige and green floral fabric cushion covers. $850

Above: Coffee table with mahogany top and center shelf.

Right: Fabric yard goods with floral design typically used for the cushions on rattan furniture and draperies, c. 1940s-1970s.

Above: Pair of rare, 3-strand, s-curve arm chairs with green floral cushions, like those that took the author nine years to collect and now fill Bruce Springsteen's Florida room. $2500. Shown with a side table and a magazine rack similar to those which follow.

Right: Triangular end table with Formica top and shelf and rattan supports. $ 425.

Far right: Contemporary rattan magazine rack. $75.

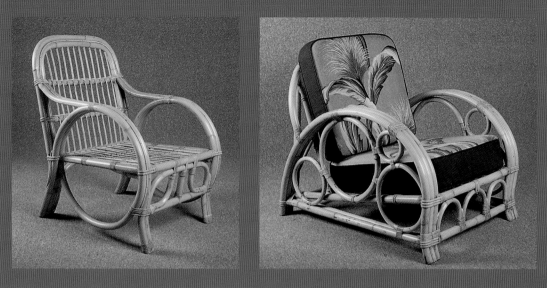

Far left: Pre-World War II rattan arm chair, shown without cushions, having two large and one small rattan strand on the continuous arms and back. Sica vertical ribs run separately in the back and seat. $625.

Left & below: Pair of triple-pole arm chairs with ring design on the sides (nicknamed the wine rack arm chair). The woman's chair has a rounded back and gray fabric with floral design. The man's chair has a straight back and cushions with black background and pink and green floral design. $975 each.

Above: Contemporary rattan round footstool with arched bent sides, round cushion missing. $225

Right: Round low table with glass top and four bent rattan legs joined by a round stretcher and resting on two rings. $320.

Fabric yard goods of floral design typically used for the cushions on rattan furniture and draperies, c. 1940s-1970s.

Round coffee table with blonde mahogany top and four curved rattan supports on round rattan base. $325. Sometimes found with a glass top. $295.

Pre-World War II living room setting from Rattan Art & Decorations, Inc., 2957 Herran Santa Ana, Manila, P.I.

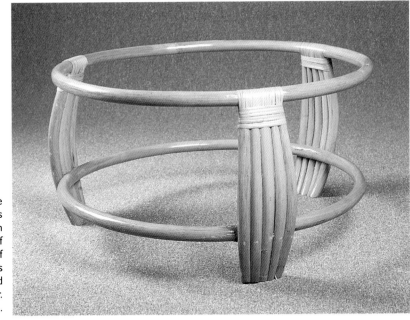

Round end table to support a glass or wood top on three bundles of five strands of rattan as legs joined by a round rattan stretcher. $525.

Above: Living room setting from Tropical Sun Rattan, Pasadena, California.

Right: Fabric yard goods of corn plant design typically used for the cushions on rattan furniture and draperies, c. 1940s-1970s.

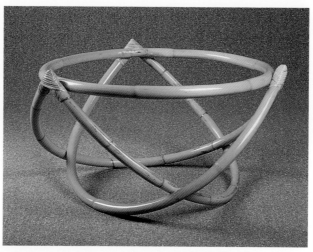

Above left: Round rattan hanging shelf unit with double round rattan frame and four horizontal pieces to support glass shelves. $240.

Above right: Round rattan "gyroscope" coffee table base for a glass top.

Right: Corner table with second level mahogany veneered top and rattan trim. $895.

Above: Pair of rattan arm chairs with arched arms on triple-strand horizontal rattan base. Seats supported by s-springs. $425 each.Rattan spiral-turned magazine rack, an example of one of the simplest rattan designs. $295.

Right: Rattan arm chair with curving arms, straight back and back ribs of sica flowing into the seat. $675.

Left: Fabric yard goods with feather design typically used for the cushions on rattan furniture and draperies, c. 1940s-1970s.

Above: End table with light Formica top and longer shelf on rattan curved supports called 3/4 pretzel. $295.

Above right: Low rattan table with freeform mahogany top and 1950s bent rattan legs.

Right: Pre-World War II rattan arm chair with continuous back and arms of three strands with pastel flamingo cushions. $975.

Above: Living room setting from Tropical Sun Rattan, Pasadena, California.

Right: Table lamp with white rectangular fabric shade on a flat stem with red background and applied rattan, resting on a rectangular base. $275.

Left: Fabric yard goods with black leopard and green tree design typically used for the cushions on rattan furniture and draperies, c. 1940s-1970s.

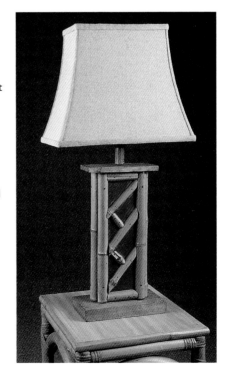

Left: Rattan arm chair with green floral sectional cushion. $875.

Center: Rectangular table with mahogany veneered top, four legs, and double box stretcher. $575.

Right: Floor lamp with stacked rattan stem and stepped round base. $895.

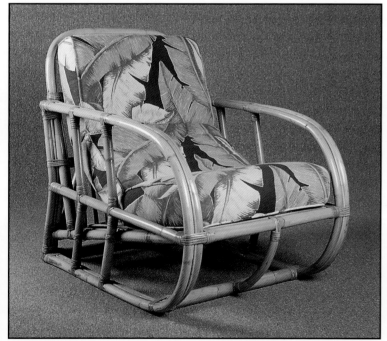

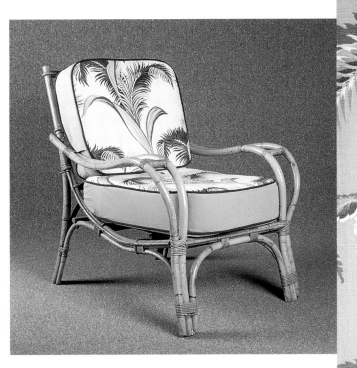

Rattan arm chair with two-strand, open scrolled arms and contemporary cushions with white background and red and green leaf design. $495.

Right: 1960s rattan arm chair with s-springs as the seat supports, arching back with two horizontal ribs, and two-strand bent arms with an extra bent piece to hold the seat cushion in place. This is an example of a free-standing base that can be used as the middle of a three-part couch or settee or as the right or left side with an arm piece attached.

Far right: Fabric yard goods with floral design typically used for the cushions on rattan furniture and draperies, c. 1940s-1970s.

Right: Low, rectangular coffee table with central raised composite painted wood shelf flanked by parallel stacked rattan shelves, resting on wrought iron legs, late 1950s, called Rod-Iron. $695.

Below: Rattan arm chair with green floral print cushions, an example of late 1950s design with no wrappings. $495.

Below right: Round stool with upholstered seat and four legs joined by round stretcher. $175.

Opposite: Pre-World War II room setting from Rattan Art & Decorations, Inc., 2957 Herran Santa Ana, Manila, P.I.

Left: Rattan arm chair with magazine racks and beverage holders built into both arms, green cushions. $595.

Right: Fabric yard goods with geometric design typically used for the cushions on rattan furniture and draperies, c. 1940s-1970s.

Below: Rattan foot stool of low rectangular form for a cushion.

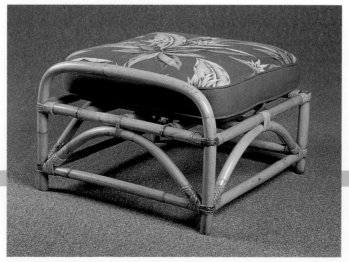

THE STYLIST

SUMMER ISSUE 1946

A MAGAZINE FOR THE HOMEMAKER

Above: Rattan ash tray stand with brown glass ash tray, square top, base of mahogany, and four straight rattan legs. $185.

Left: Cover of the magazine *The Stylist*, 1946, showing rattan furniture.

Above: Living room setting from Tropical Sun Rattan, Pasadena, California.

Left: Fabric yard goods of floral design typically used for the cushions on rattan furniture and draperies, c. 1940s-1970s.

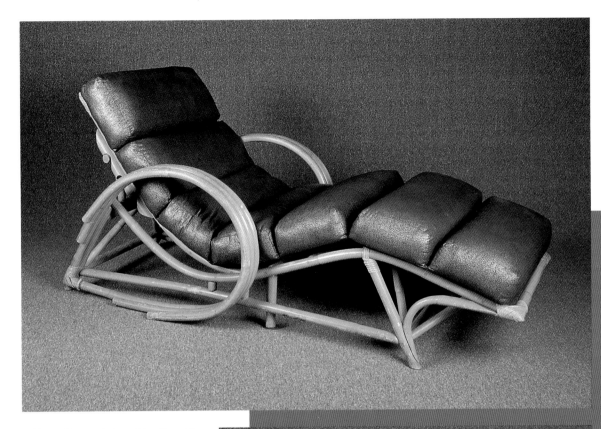

Above: Rattan chaise with adjustable back and staggered bent rattan arms forming a tear drop, with gray and black sectional cushion. $1600.

Right: Mahogany veneer and rattan open bookshelves. $450.

Far right: Table lamp with rectangular green fabric shade and green reeds on a rectangular stem. $285.

Pre-World War
II living room
setting from
Rattan Art &
Decorations,
Inc., 2957
Herran Santa
Ana, Manila, P.I.

Rattan chaise, 1951, with three-strand arm and brace at foot. $1600

Round rattan dining table with glass top, rattan trim, and four raking, stacked rattan supports that curve inward to join a small ring stretcher. Legs similarly curve outward to form four legs.

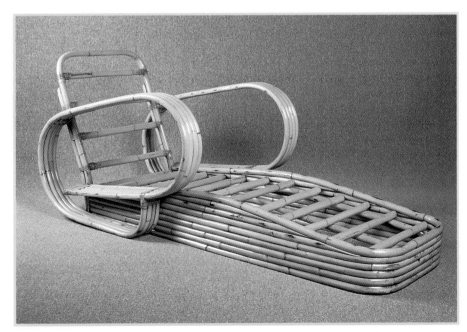

Rattan lounge with continuous curved arms, arching back with five horizontal ribs, and raised seat with added, hand-tapered poles at the middle. $1800.

Contemporary rattan chaise with continuous curved poles. $795.

RATTAN IN THE DINING ROOM

Above: Large rectangular rattan table with the ironwood top missing and four rattan arm chairs. Table $1250, chairs $325 each.

Right: Dining room setting from Tropical Sun Rattan, Pasadena, California.

Opposite: Pre-World War II dining room setting from Rattan Art & Decorations, Inc., 2957 Herran Santa Ana, Manila, P.I.

Color print "Festival of the Sea" by Eugene Savage, commissioned by the Matson Navigation Company of San Francisco, c. 1946, and used on menu covers during the voyages to Hawaii.

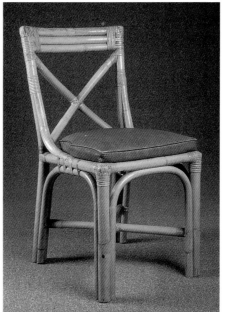

Above: Dining room setting from Tropical Sun Rattan, Pasadena, California.

Left: Side chair of rattan frame with x-crossing in the back and cushioned seat, the most usual design. $295

Far left: Three-panel folding screen with bamboo frame and woven reed hung in the panels. $120.

Above: Rattan extension table with light wood grain Formica top and four stacked rattan legs. $925.

Left: Two part glass front cabinet and two-door base with woven grass covering and sica. $1400.

Five-color print of Hawaiian people by Frank MacIntosh commissioned in the 1930s by the Matson Navigation Company of San Francisco for use on menu covers during the voyages to Hawaii.

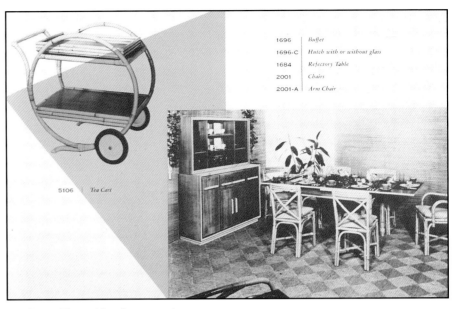

1696	Buffet
1696-C	Hutch with or without glass
1684	Refectory Table
2001	Chairs
2001-A	Arm Chair

5106 | Tea Cart

Page from a Tropical Sun Rattan catalog, 1963, with designs by Jerry Johnson.

Low end table with square, wood grain Formica top, rattan edge, and two supports of four-strand rattan on a curving base board. $175.

Opposite: Pre-World War II dining room setting from Rattan Art & Decorations, Inc., 2957 Herran Santa Ana, Manila, P.I.

Right: Square draw-leaf table with mahogany top, straight skirt and four stacked rattan legs. $1295.

Far right: Heavy three-panel folding screen of rattan with three open trellis-work panels and a vertical rattan stacked base in each. $725.

Below: Rattan dining table with rectangular mahogany top with rounded corners, resting on two triangular rattan stacks. $1800.

Armoire cabinet with sica frame and grass mat covering; five shelves on each side of two solid doors on a base of cedar. $1650.

Rattan and light wood cabinet with rectangular top, curved corners, two drawers and two doors. $1200.

Five-color print of Hawaiian people by Frank MacIntosh commissioned in the 1930s by the Matson Navigation Company of San Francisco for use on menu covers during the voyages to Hawaii.

Dining table with dark wood rectangular top
over two oval stacks of rattan. $2800.

Half-round stacked rattan supports for a
desk or dining table top, about 30" high.

Rattan extension table with brown wood grain Formica
top and two supports of stacked rattan. $695.

Rattan cabinet with mahogany top and fronts, bent rattan
poles at the sides, two drawers and two doors. $1800.

Large framed painting of two flamingos, signed
Seay, an artist for Turner Manufacturing. $1200.

Above right: Side chair with basketweave sica-
covered back and seat and bent oak and spindle
carved straight legs and crossing stretcher. $325.

Lower right: Square table with rounded corners,
wood veneer top, and four wicker legs. $1295.

Left: Rattan dining table and matching chairs designed by Henry Olko, 1981.

Lower left: Serving cabinet with rectangular top of wood with rattan trim, one drawer, and two doors with rattan pulls. $800.

Lower right: Rattan cabinet with mahogany top and fronts, straight rattan poles at the sides, two drawers and two doors. $1800.

Above & left: Rattan drop-leaf table with a Formica wood grain top and side chair of matching looped rattan legs with black vinyl seat covering. Table $950, chairs $225 each.

Far left: Fabric yard goods of floral design typically used for the cushions on rattan furniture and draperies, c. 1940s-1970s.

Picture 1 Dining chair 4250-2200 and Dining table 4060-4800. Picture 2 Hi-back lounge chair 4250-5500. Picture 3 Coffee table/tempered glass 4684-3000.

Catalog page with rattan tables and chairs.

Above: Square rattan table with mahogany top on four stacked rattan legs and arm chairs with sweeping rattan frames. Table $695, chairs $325 each.

Left: Contemporary four-shelf unit of mahogany and rattan frame, two cabinet doors with sica trim. $795.

105

Above: 1938 dining room setting from Tropical Sun Rattan, Pasadena, California.

Right: Fabric yard goods of abstract geometric design typically used for the cushions on rattan furniture and draperies, c. 1940s-1970s.

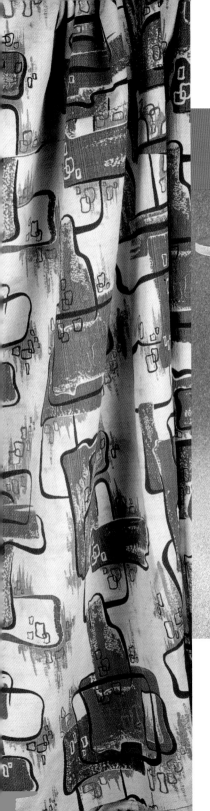

Above: Round rattan center table with black painted wood top and six bent sections joined by rings at the top and bottom.

Above right: Round table with cowhide top on a drum shaped base of stacked rattan. $700.

Right: Hollow rattan cylinder with stacked rings of bent rattan for a single or double pedestal dining table, about 30" high.

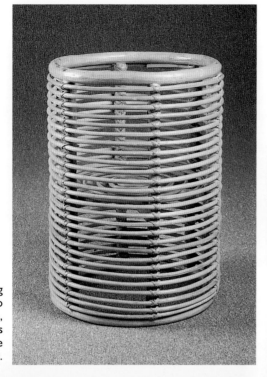

Drum-shaped dining table base of rattan to support a glass top, with coiled sica lengths on the crossing middle support. $200.

Low round table with mahogany veneered top. $595.

Rattan-covered cylinder base with two wooden ends used as the base for a dining table.

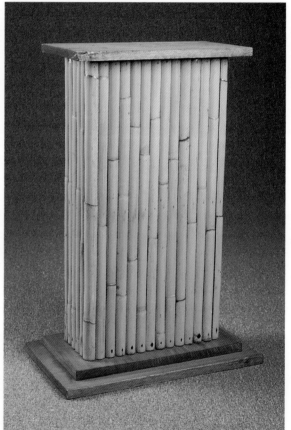

Rattan pedestal for a dining table with a stepped rectangular mahogany base and stacked rattan rectangular pillar with overhanging mahogany plank to support a separate top. $620.

Pre-World War II barroom setting from Rattan Art & Decorations, Inc., 2957 Herran Santa Ana, Manila, P.I.

RATTAN IN THE BARROOM

Rattan hanging shelf with seven-strand, stacked rattan frame and four slits to support two louvered glass shelves, with decal label "Kane Kraft & Rattan Art Decorations Inc. —Herran— Manila." $375.

Rattan bar with light wood grain Formica top and horizontal stacked rattan wrapping around a canted front, both arm and foot rests are projecting. $1750.

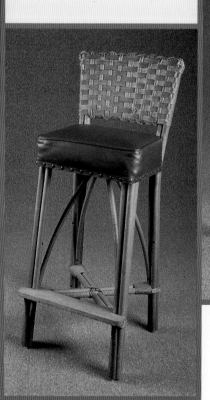

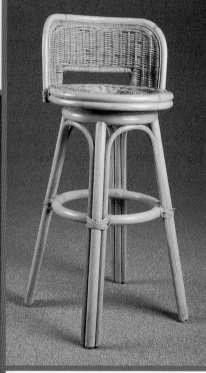

1980s bar stool of rattan with wicker back and round seat. $120.

1940s bar stool with rattan rectangular back and deep red vinyl upholstered seat on stacked ribbed oak legs with foot rest and crossing, ribbed-post stretcher.

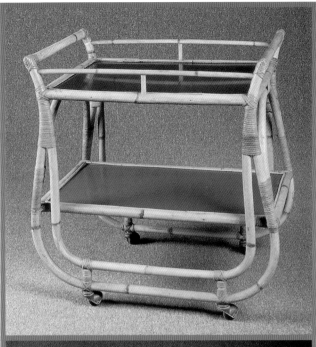

Serving cart with two black rectangular shelves in rattan frames, resting on castors. $235.

Three-panel folding screen with rattan frame and diagonal weave in the panels. $395.

Serving cart with a stacked rattan facing on two deep compartments with hinged lids, light wood grain Formica lining, and castors. $500.

Above: Bar stool with white upholstered round seat and label "Tropical Sun Company, Pasadena, California." $325.

Left: 1938 barroom setting from Tropical Sun Rattan, Pasadena, California.

Above: Hanging shelf unit with slanted roof pieces. Labeled with decal "Calif-Asia quality rattan furniture, 6818 Avalon Blvd. Los Angles. Made in the Philippines." $295.

Right: Rectangular rattan serving tray. $75.

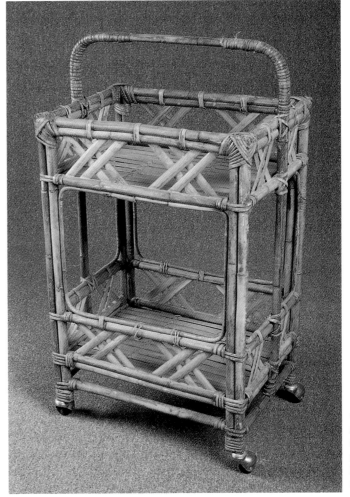

Contemporary serving cart of rattan and split slats, rectangular tray and lower shelf, on castors. $300.

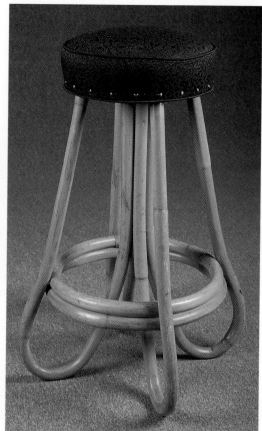

Bar with mahogany top and front covered in raffia weave, with projecting foot rail on shaped wooden feet. Bar stool with round, red cushioned seat. Bar $1800.

Above right: 1950s rattan bar stool with dark red upholstered seat and four looped legs joined by a double ring foot rest. $325.

Right: Serving cart with removable rectangular tray and mahogany veneered base, matching lower tray, curved, rattan feet, and two wheels. $750.

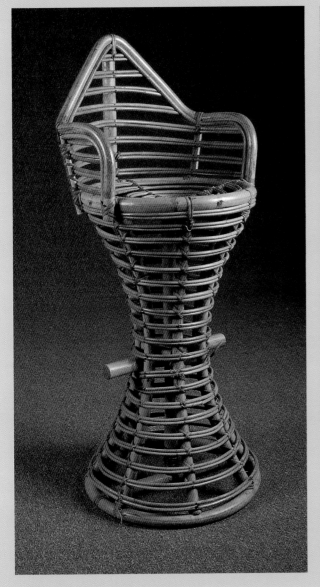

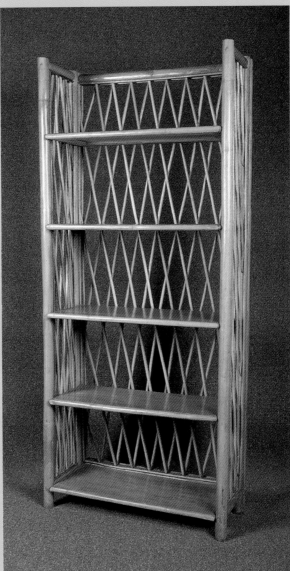

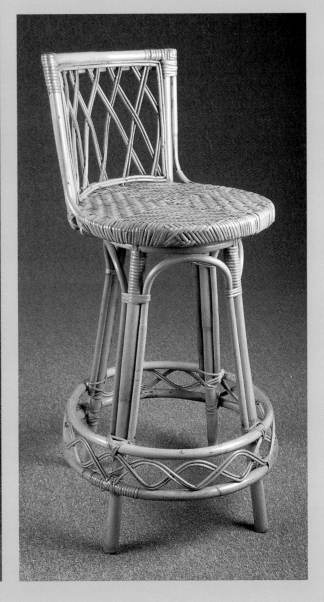

Bar stool with rattan frame, round
seat, and horizontal sica ribs. $325.

Contemporary five-shelf unit with mahogany shelves
and crossing rattan on the sides and back. $495.

1980s bar stool with rectangular back and crossing
wicker ribs, woven mat over round seat. $225.

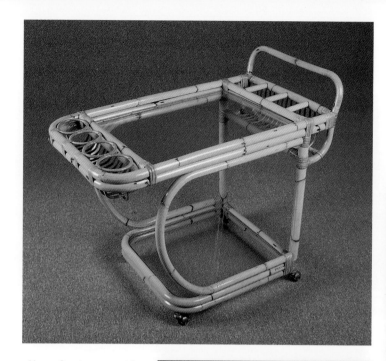

Above: Serving cart with two glass shelves, rattan frame and two wells with sica ribs for extra items, resting on castors. $425.

Right: Bar stool with rectangular back of rattan and woven mat covered round seat. $325.

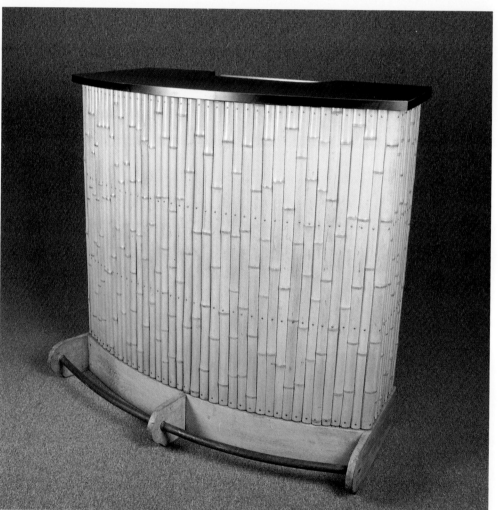

Rattan bar with black Formica top and the front faced with stacked rattan. A brass footrest projects from the wooden base. $1595.

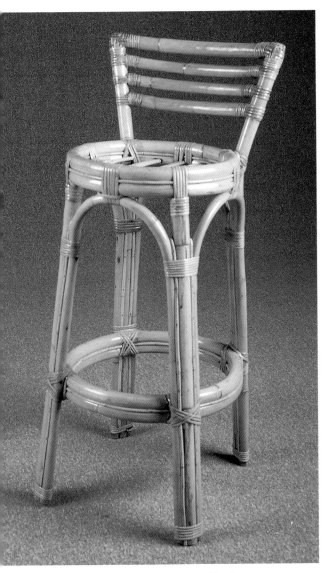

Early bar stool with four horizontal back slats of rattan and round seat. $325.

Bar stool with rattan frame and basket seat on four legs with round stretcher. $285.

Bar stool with rattan back and legs, red upholstered round seat, labeled "Ritts Co. Original Fine Casual Furniture, Los Angeles, 64."

Above: Bar with three mirrored panels and horizontal stacked rattan, mahogany top. $1200.

Right: Bar stool with green vinyl curving back and seat on four three-strand rattan legs and a continuous pole ring stretcher. $320.

Contemporary four-panel folding screen of rattan with six open areas on each panel and four sets of framed corners on each panel. $295.

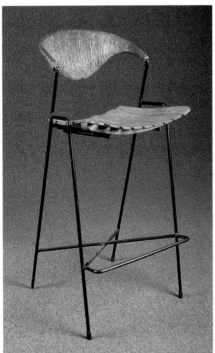

Above: Serving cart with rectangular light wood grain Formica top and shelf in rattan frame on castors. $575.

Right: Bar stool with curving twisted paper wrap back, wrought iron frame, and slatted seat. $245.

Five-shelf unit. $595.

119

Left: Bar stool with straight paper wrap back, wrought iron frame, and slatted seat. $245.

Below: Serving cart with oval top tray of dark Formica, crossing side rails, and woven lower shelf, on casters. $525.

Old bamboo open shelves with rectangular top overhanging the grass mat covered case where three long shelves rest over four bamboo legs. $750.

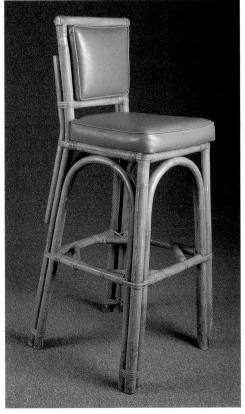

Left & below: Coffee table or pumpkin bar, a low round table with vertical rattan facing which splits open vertically to expose interior shelves and a drawer. The pumpkin form rests on castors. $925.

Bar stool with rattan frame and green vinyl upholstered square back and seat on rattan legs. $265.

RATTAN IN THE LIBRARY

Pre-World War II library
setting from Rattan Art
& Decorations, Inc.,
2957 Herran Santa Ana,
Manila, P.I.

Color print of tropical flowers signed by Tip Freeman, Honolulu.

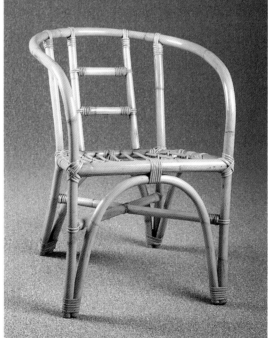

Above: Flat top knee-hole desk with mahogany top and case faced with vertical rattan, three drawers in each side case flanking the center drawer. $1700.

Left: Rattan arm chair with continuous bent arms and back, D-shaped seat, and crossing stretcher. $395.

Square rattan waste basket/plant
holder about 12" high.

Contemporary four-shelf unit with open
back, rattan frame, glass shelves, and
square side spaces. $595.

Above: Desk of light wood grain Formica panels in a rattan frame with three open shelves on the left side, a center drawer, and four drawers on the right side with rattan handles. $950.

Left: Fabric yard goods with floral design typically used for the cushions on rattan furniture and draperies, c. 1940s-1970s.

Three-panel folding screen of rattan and openwork sica in a geometric pattern. $1125.

Rattan desk with mahogany top and woven rice stalk covering on the front and sides of one long drawer, two side drawers, and a plank leg. $795.

1930s floor lamp with woven wicker shade, rattan arm and stacked stem that flares to join the round wooden base. $595.

Opposite: Pre-World War II library setting from Rattan Art & Decorations, Inc., 2957 Herran Santa Ana, Manila, P.I.

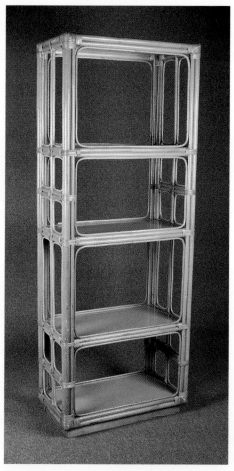

Contemporary rattan shelf unit with rectangular spaces in the open sides and four Formica rectangular shelves. $375.

Framed painting of pink birds, signed Jessie Arms Botke.

Table lamp with double round parchment shade on rattan stem and four curved ribs bound by raffia on a round base. $235.

128

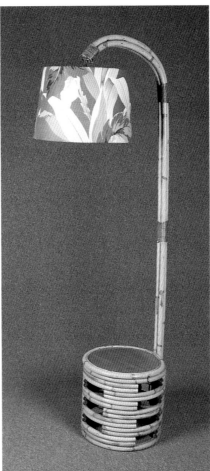

Floor lamp with green fabric shade hanging from a crooked rattan pole above a round drum base with mahogany top and staggered rattan stacked sides. The base opens to expose a rack for bottles.

Above: Rattan arm chair with continuous curved back and arms, seat upholstered in brown vinyl, rattan legs joined by a crossing stretcher. $325.

Right: Three rattan waste baskets. $125 to 225.

129

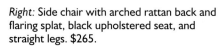

Right: Side chair with arched rattan back and flaring splat, black upholstered seat, and straight legs. $265.

Far right: Standing floor lamp with round parchment shade on a long stacked rattan and sica stem and stepped wooden base. $495.

Below: Desk with mahogany rectangular top over single drawer on straight rattan legs and a rattan screen on the back and sides. $1275.

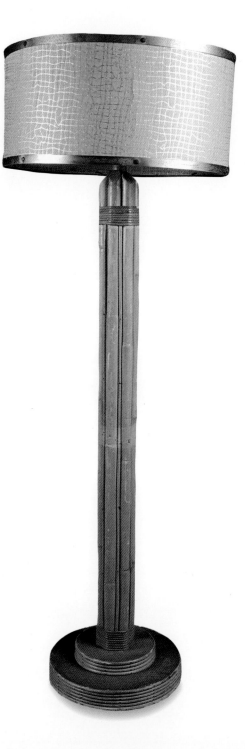

Left: Mahogany veneer and rattan table with three rectangular shelves and open woven reed in the base skirt. $475.

Below: Painting of pink birds, signed Seay, an artist for Turner Manufacturing. $795.

Above: Rattan side chair from the Trader Vic's restaurant chain with rectangular back, cushioned Naugahyde seat, and straight rattan legs. $325.

Left: Small old bamboo writing desk with pine wood, grass mat covered box with interior compartments and hinged fall front writing surface. A single drawer in the case has a grass mat front and bamboo handle resting over four bamboo legs and side braces. $895.

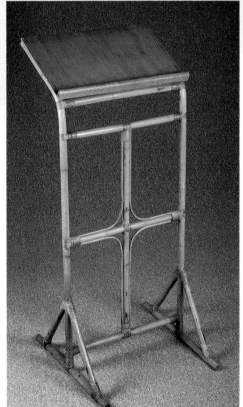

Above: Rattan rectangular wall shelf unit with stacked roof over two Formica shelves and rattan supports, 1950s. $275.

Left: Lectern on tall base with slanted shelf. $400.

1960s bamboo, four-panel folding screen with vertical reed mat panels and contrasting black vine decoration in the open, arching top, about 48" high. $275.

RATTAN IN THE BEDROOM

Bedroom setting from Tropical Sun Rattan, Pasadena, California.

Above: Night stand or end table of two drawers over one door, with mahogany top and fronts and rattan sides and base. $575.

Opposite: Pre-World War II bedroom setting from Rattan Art & Decorations, Inc., 2957 Herran Santa Ana, Manila, P.I.

Five-color printed menu cover of Hawaiian people by Frank MacIntosh in the 1930s for the Matson Navigation Company of San Francisco for use during the voyages to Hawaii.

Left: Rattan ceiling fixture for a barrel light, cylinder of coiled sica. $180.

Below: Rattan side chair with rectangular back of eight posts, cushioned seat. $220.

Opposite: Pre-World War II bedroom setting from Rattan Art & Decorations, Inc., 2957 Herran Santa Ana, Manila, P.I.

Pre-World War II
bedroom setting
from Rattan Art &
Decorations, Inc.,
2957 Herran Santa
Ana, Manila, P.I.

Above: Chest of drawers with mahogany top, curved corners, and two drawers over three long drawers with mahogany fronts and rattan sides. $1600.

Right: Rattan and mahogany armoire and cabinet with tall clothespress with hanging bar and shelves next to four drawers with metal and rattan pulls. $4500.

Large tiki-hut-
shaped table
lamp of woven
mats in flat
frames. $350.

Above: Bedroom setting from Tropical Sun Rattan, Pasadena, California.

Left: Fabric yard goods with floral design typically used for the cushions on rattan furniture and draperies, c. 1940s-1970s.

Right: Large rectangular mirror in five-pole rattan frame. $450

Right: Table lamp with two small burlap round shades and curving rattan posts on a rectangular base with copper-lined plan container. $300.

Below left: Fan rattan single bed with curved head board and straight foot board. $900.

Below right: Mahogany and rattan chest of three drawers with rattan pulls. $1100.

Dressing table and bench of rattan, two side cases with three drawers in each. $1200.

Above: Two matching, contemporary, three-panel folding screens with four woven mat panels, one screen with parrot pattern wallpaper on one side. Each $295.

Above right: Bedroom setting from Tropical Sun Rattan, Pasadena, California.

Right: Mahogany and rattan chest of three drawers with horizontal rattan pulls. $800.

Two dressing tables with mahogany tops and rattan cases, each with three drawers flanking the center drawer, nice examples of tight, bent corners. $1800 each.

Above: Mahogany and rattan night stand or end table with rectangular top over an open shelf and low drawer. $375.

Left: Rattan dressing table with sica and woven mat covering, a large round mirror attached above the case, and two stacks of two drawers flanking a low shelf. $900.

Right: Rattan side chair with upholstered seat in print fabric. $195.

Above: Mahogany chest of four drawers with rattan pulls and base. $1450.

Right: Pre-World War II three-panel folding rattan screen with higher center section, arched panels, and woven mat panels. $875.

147

Above: Two side chairs of rattan frame with upholstered seats. $325.

Right: Fabric yard goods of leaf design typically used for the cushions on rattan furniture and draperies, c. 1940s-1970s.

Above: Night stand or end table with mahogany veneered frame and rattan front edging, enclosing three shelves. $1800.

Left: Floor lamp/table with white glass globe, green shade, and hinged metal arm, rattan stem, round Formica shelf and base. $575.

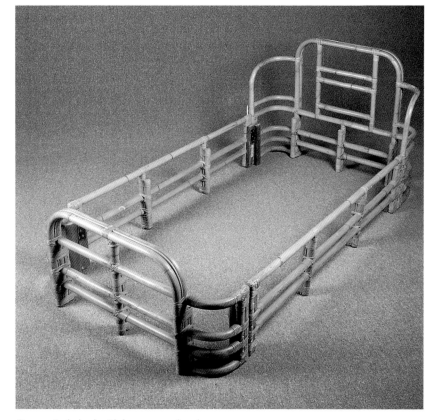

Rattan single bed with bent rattan head and foot boards and straight sides. $900.

149

Right: Tall chest of five drawers with wooden panels and rattan frame and pulls. This is a hand-made sample for Tropical Sun Rattan of Pasadena, California, from the 1950s.

Far right: Four-panel folding screen with bamboo frame, parrot wallpaper on one side and woven reed mat on the other. $875.

150

Chest of drawers with light wood grain Formica panels in a rattan frame and two small over three long drawers with rattan pulls. $750.

Low cabinet with light wood grain Formica panels in rattan frame, two hinged doors with rattan handles. $350.

Rattan night stand or end table with light wood grain Formica panels, single drawer over two shelves lined with woven grass cloth. $275.

151

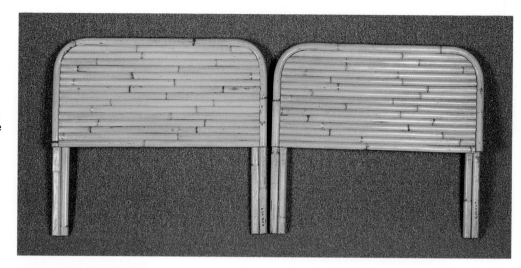

Right: Head and foot boards for a twin sized bed with horizontal rattan stacked in a two-strand rattan frame with curving corners. This is unused stock from the 1950s.

Below left: Bedroom setting from Tropical Sun Rattan, Pasadena, California.

Below right: Night stand or end table with mahogany top and three drawers, and rattan trim between the drawers and stacked in the base. $425.

Rattan shoe rack with two slanted
shelves and flat bottom shelf. $250.

Above: Contemporary rattan cheval
looking glass in frame with arched
mirrored glass panel. $595.

Right: Floor lamp/table with rattan stem
and light wood grain Formica square table
top and base with rattan legs. $375.

Above: Rattan vanity with mahogany shelf recessed between two stacks of three drawers.

Left: Menu cover "Aloha" by Frank MacIntosh commissioned by the Matson Navigation Company of San Francisco for use during the voyages to Hawaii, 1930s.

Above left: Rattan side chair with arching back and crossing pieces making nine open squares. The seat is upholstered over a frame and rests on straight legs with arching braces and a crossing stretcher. $325.

Left: Contemporary rattan standing shelf of double hoop shape on down-curved legs enclosing open cross-shaped rattan shelving. $75.

Above right: 1930s four-panel folding screen of woven flat reed in light and dark shades of brown and geometric pattern. The panel tops are squared at 45-degree angles. $1200.

155

RATTAN FOR CHILDREN

Above: Child's bedroom setting from Tropical Sun Rattan, Pasadena, California.

Right: Child's rectangular desk and seat of mahogany joined by rattan supports on a rectangular base, made for Rows. $250.

Right: Child's rattan side chair with basketweave seat and rattan ribs in the back. $295.

Far right: Rattan and mahogany child's low dressing table with round mirror in a rattan frame over a shaped top and case with center drawer flanked by two drawers on each side. $975.

Below: Child's rocking arm chair with three-strand stacked bent arms and rockers. $975.

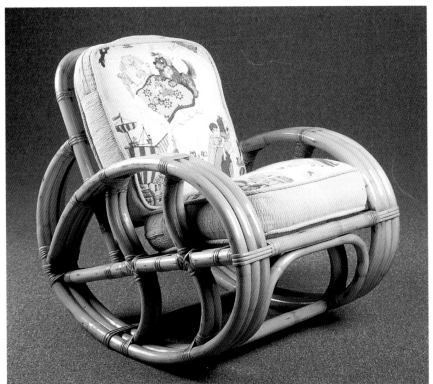

Above left: Child's rattan ship with chair seat. $325.

Above right: Early and rare child's chair with bent rattan continuous back and arms. $395.

Right: Child's 1950s, four-piece rattan set of table, two chairs, and settee. All with white painted rattan frames and bright floral-covered cushions. The table has a yellow vinyl top cover. Children's furniture from the period is very valuable, and would be more valuable not painted. Settee $600, chairs $300 each, table $100.

INDEX

ABOUT THE AUTHOR

Harvey Schwartz has applied his interest in product designs to each phase of his career. In 1959, when the space race began, he worked on space-related products. When contracts ran out in 1969, he turned to his growing collections of memorabilia and opened an antique store on Third Street near Beverly Boulevard in Los Angeles. Besides general merchandise, he was attracted to forms of Art Deco design. Business grew and by the early 1970s he moved to a store on Melrose Avenue and began providing Art Deco furniture to movie stars and other fashionable clients. Barbra Streisand was a good customer who furnished her main house with Art Deco and her guest house at the beach with Harvey's rattan furniture.

Searching for more rattan than he found in the antiques trade, Harvey discovered Tropical Sun Rattan Company in Pasadena, California. This company was then selling awnings and wrought iron furniture but had a warehouse of old stock rattan furniture still in its import packing boxes. The stock included all sorts of rattan designs, from the two-strand, arm varieties to the full twelve-strand, pretzel-arm styles which are very rare. Harvey arranged to buy the whole rattan inventory and the rights to use the name Tropical Sun Rattan. In 1978, a second store was opened, on Main Street in Santa Monica, specializing in rattan furniture. Here the 4,000 square foot showroom was set up in room settings; at the time it was the largest display of antique rattan in the world.

As in the movies, the good times lasted only a short time. The eight-month screen writers' and actors' strikes in 1980 brought Hollywood to its knees, and Harvey backed down to one store, the one on Melrose Avenue, where he presented his general merchandise and a big display of vintage rattan. Besides selling his antiques, Harvey rented them to the studios for specific projects.

In 1982, rattan from Harvey was featured on the sets of a new program for television, "The Golden Girls." The instant and long-lasting success of this show launched new interest in rattan furniture nationally. Without realizing why, the show's audience was attracted to rattan for their own homes, and Harvey's business took another leap forward. As he progressed in his business with the Hollywood studios, Harvey opened a prop house he called 20th Century Props to concentrate on providing rented interior furnishings. His business in props skyrocketed. In 1994, the Melrose Avenue store was closed so that all his effort could be put into renting props. Today, 20th Century Props is one of the three largest prop businesses in the world.

But with all his success, Harvey has not abandoned rattan. Tropical Sun Rattan is still listed in the phone book and he will still sell or rent you a piece or enough for a whole room, a house, a hotel or restaurant. Harvey knows rattan from the bottom up.